Little Kitty
the Cat Burglar

To dear Rayner

With best wishes

Susan x

A message from
Alzheimer's Research UK

All the proceeds from this delightful book are being donated towards our vital work at Alzheimer's Research UK to prevent, treat and cure dementia. Everyone who buys a copy of *Little Kitty the Cat Burglar* will bring us closer to our vision of a world where people are free from the fear, harm and heartbreak of Alzheimer's disease and other forms of dementia.

We are hugely grateful to the many people involved in compiling and producing this book for making that possible.

Hilary Evans, Chief Executive, Alzheimer's Research UK, the UK's leading dementia research charity. www.alzheimersresearchuk.org

This book has been written to raise funds for
Alzheimer's Research UK

To learn more about Alzheimer's Research UK, visit:
www.alzheimersresearchuk.org

Many thanks to these lovely people for
giving their free time and skills:

Writers: Tracy Terry, Ann Bowyer, Suzan Collins, Lucille Rayner,
Jo Wilde, Tottie Limejuice, JB Johnston, and Ros Lyons

Illustrator: Catie Atkinson

Designer: Rachel Lawston

Editor: Jaine Keskeys

Published by SPC Publishing UK in 2015

British Library Cataloguing in Publication Data.

A CIP catalogue record for this book is available from
the British Library.

ISBN: 978-0-9931690-7-6

Little Kitty
the Cat Burglar

Caterina Longtail

Chapter One

Ah, how I love Sunday mornings! Sunday is positively my second favourite day of the week. Fridays are my favourite, when I always have fresh fish for dinner.

A tray of tea and buttery toast has already been devoured I see. With a bit of luck there will be a smear or two of delicious butter left on the plate for me to lick clean.

My humans are still in bed, with

newspapers and various magazines spread over the quilt. He'll be reading the latest international news; she'll be looking at the weekly book reviews.

Perhaps later, with the weather being so unseasonably warm, they'll head off to some car boot sale or – my fur bristles at the very thought – a . . . a . . . a flea market.

And what does this Sunday have in store for me? Tired of having my tummy tickled, even in the spot that makes me purr in delight, and uninterested in pouncing on toes wiggling beneath the bedclothes, I leisurely wander outside into Peppercorn Place.

I sit on the wall of the Victorian terrace, most of its houses long since converted into flats. The autumn sun, low in the sky, warms my fur and I sniff in the scent of roasting meat, of Yorkshire puddings, of . . . I would add vegetables boiling in their pans, but what self-respecting feline would admit to liking broccoli?

Whoa! Roasting meats? That can only mean one thing.

Thunk!

I'm soon racing through the cat flap, over the newly tiled kitchen floor and up the stairs, dragging my prized possession with me.

Oh my, this is proving to be much harder work than I'd anticipated. I stop for a rest, nonchalantly licking my paws, cleaning my whiskers and behind my ears. Let's hope she-human appreciates all my efforts.

She hasn't been very pleased with my other gifts. For example, she didn't exactly jump for joy when I brought home that mouse. Yes, she did *jump*, but it was with fright onto the nearest chair. And then there was the time I brought home that sparrow ... Well, the less said about that the better.

I just hope she'll be more grateful for the piece of beef, still warm from the oven, that was recently liberated – I won't use the word 'stolen'; I refuse to think of myself as a cat burglar – from the kitchen of Mrs Browne, our elderly neighbour, and oh-so-daringly carried up the stairs.

Chapter Two

I'm all alone today. My humans didn't come back on Sunday – it seems they have gone on holiday. As I laze on the back of the sofa, basking in the autumn sunshine streaming through the window, I wonder if I should visit Mrs Browne. She might be feeling lonely, too.

I stretch and arch my back before jumping down and wandering into

5

the kitchen. My food bowl is empty. Mrs Browne fed me this morning, but maybe I will nip over the wall and remind her that it's time for my dinner now.

As the cat flap clatters behind me, I climb the fence. A quick look down tells me it's safe and I'm soon heading towards Mrs Browne's back door. Unfortunately, I don't notice that the side gate is open and, at the precise moment I arrive at the door, a large black dog appears.

We stare at each other. I spit my anger. He has no right to be there! He growls and lunges forward. I turn and sprint up the nearest tree, and he barks and dances round its trunk.

Mrs Browne soon comes out to see what all the fuss is about. She yells at the dog and, to my surprise, it quickly retreats up the garden towards the house. Mrs Browne follows and slams the back door shut behind them, leaving me clinging to a slender branch.

When I decide to climb down, I discover I'm stuck. I meow and meow but it's a very long time before Mrs Browne comes back out again.

"Are you still up there, you silly Little Kitty?" she says, staring up at me. "Come on, down you climb."

I'm not silly. There's no way I'm risking my neck! And anyway, I'm not sure if the dog is still around . . .

Mrs Browne goes back indoors and then returns with a bowl of my favourite food – fish. But I just can't risk moving on this weak branch.

"You silly, silly Little Kitty. I guess I'll have to go and get Fred," she tells me when I still don't climb down.

I meow and meow until a man arrives with a ladder. He leans it against the tree, then climbs up and tries to reach me.

"It's no good. I can't get her." Fred climbs back down. "You'll just have to call the fire brigade," he tells Mrs Browne.

It seems like a very long time passes, then I hear Mrs Browne thanking the firemen for arriving so quickly. One of the firemen places a long ladder – much longer than Fred's – against the tree and he is soon up beside my branch, coaxing me towards him. I meow even louder. I can't turn round!

Suddenly, he makes a grab for me. I scratch at his arms, digging in my claws. I spit and screech, unhappy at the way he's holding me, but his grip only tightens as he descends the ladder.

The fireman places me gently on the ground and I don't hesitate. Fish or no fish, I'm not hanging around! It's much safer in my own home.

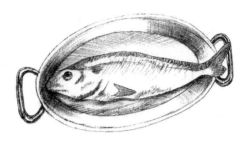

Chapter Three

I put my ears back and run. I shoot through the cat flap and skid across the polished floor. *Wheeeeee!*

I sit for a moment and sniff the air. No new smells in here. So I walk into the lounge and lay on the sofa to enjoy the peace and quiet.

I raise one of my back legs and start to lick it. Then I remember that it's Monday, and I always work on my front paws on Mondays. I nip at my claws, but only a little. They can't be too short – I need them to scratch things and to grip onto tree trunks when I'm climbing.

Ah, trees! I remember now. I only went out to get some food, but then I got frightened by that big dog and had to run up a tree to safety.

I can hear the front door opening. It must be time for my feed, so I run to the door as fast as I can. I was right – it's Mrs Browne and I smell fish!

"Did that big nasty dog frighten you, Little Kitty?"

"Of course not! I was just respecting his space, that's all," I tell her with a flick of my tail. "Is that food for me?"

"No need to be scared, I'm here now. And it's time for your dinner. I told your mama I would feed you while she's away on holiday."

"Come on then, put it down," I say, pointing my nose towards the ground. But she doesn't, so I start meowing and walking in between her legs, going round and round in circles.

She walks round in circles, too, and laughs. "You're making me dizzy!"

"Put the food down then, please."

I watch her take the cover off the food and place the bowl on the floor. I rush towards it and start eating. Mmmm, fish. Probably haddock. I usually prefer fresh salmon, even cod, but this is fine for today. I begin to purr as I eat.

When I've finished I look up at Mrs Browne and ask, "Have you got any more? Please?"

"Finished already? Well, that's it for today I'm afraid. I'll bring some more another time."

"In about thirty minutes?" I ask cheekily, rubbing against her legs.

"Stop looking at me like that, Little Kitty. Your mama said I should only feed you twice a day."

"Pretty please!" I purr.

"Oh, you're so sweet. But I really mustn't give you more food today."

"But she won't know! She's not here." I lick her hand.

"Stop making me feel guilty, Little Kitty. When your mama's back I'll have to tell her how cheeky you've been, pestering me like this!"

I stop licking and look up at Mrs Browne. I talk to her because she's lonely, but now she says that she'll tell tales on me! With that, I point my long tail straight up, raise my nose in the air and then walk over to my litter tray.

Chapter Four

I don't want to go outside to the toilet. I had too much of a fright out there earlier, what with the dog, the tree and the fireman, when all I wanted was my fish dinner. So now Mrs Browne can clean my litter tray before she leaves with the empty food bowl.

Mrs Browne looks at me and says, "There you are, Little Kitty. A nice big bowl of fresh water. Oh, and I guess I had better clean your litter tray before I go."

I purr. I knew she would.

"Bye, now," says Mrs Browne. "See you in the morning." She closes the door behind her.

Ah! A nice peaceful house again. I think it's time to curl up for a sleep. My humans' bed is very comfortable, so up the stairs I shall go.

BANG. BANG. THUMP! BANG. BANG. THUMP!

Opening my eyes and stretching out, I wonder what all the noise is. With one last big stretch, I jump off the bed and onto the window ledge. It's morning! I have slept all night! The new neighbours on the other side are working in their garden. It looks like a building site. I'll explore it later.

I hear the front door open and a voice calls, "Hello, Little Kitty!"

Oh, it's Mrs Browne, and she's brought my breakfast with her.

I race down the stairs and slide across the floor, purring as I go. I smell chicken and a nice bowl of milk. Looking at Mrs Browne, I meow, "Put my food down, please. I'm hungry."

"There you go, Little Kitty," says Mrs Browne, doing as I ask.

I tuck in and soon both bowls are licked clean. "Yum!" I say, before cleaning my paws and whiskers.

I purr to show Mrs Browne that I am grateful for the food. Then I go through the cat flap and into the garden.

Looking through a hole in the fence into the new neighbours' building site, there are no humans in sight. It must be the humans' drinking time, I think. Time to explore!

There are lots of things that humans use to make houses, and a big noisy machine is turning round and round. Oh, and what's this? A smooth, shiny new surface to walk on.

Meow! It's wet and my feet are sinking into it!

I don't like to get my feet wet, so I quickly run and jump up onto the fence. As I sit there looking back at where I've just been, I see that my paw prints are all over the wet stuff. Oops! I think I'd better hide.

Back in my garden I curl up under a bush and snooze, until I hear shouting from next door. I keep still and listen.

"Sandra, just come and have a look at this. There are paw prints on our new path! I bet it was that ginger cat from next door."

How on earth could he possibly know it was *me*? I mean, it could have been any cat! It doesn't say 'The ginger cat was here'.

Sandra replies: "Yes, Bill, that cat does come in the garden sometimes. But, really, it could have been any cat."

I purr. Exactly.

Now, I'd better make sure my paws are cleaned properly, so there's no evidence to show that it was me, the ginger cat . . .

Chapter Five

I must have fallen asleep. When I wake up, I see a huge black tomcat sitting on the fence. He's looking at me, and not in a very friendly way.

"Is this your house?" he asks. "Is there any food? Do you have a human? Are the beds comfortable?"

I'm puzzled by all these sudden questions and take my time thinking about how to reply.

"Come on, stupid!" says the intruder rather impatiently. "What's up? Cat got your tongue?"

Well, I don't find that particularly amusing, but he's obviously pretty pleased with himself. He jumps off the fence and slowly strolls up to me, staring right into my eyes the whole time.

"*Yes-s-s-s*, this is my house," I hiss at him, bristling. "My house, my food, my humans and my beds."

I take a step towards him to show that I'm not scared, but he stays where he is. Hmm. This could turn nasty if I'm not careful. I don't want a fight – I prefer to keep my good looks unscratched.

"I'll just take a look around," he says, sauntering off towards the cat flap.

What am I supposed to do now?

Where is Mrs Browne when I need her? She'd be able to get rid of this big-headed newcomer. I look hopefully towards the gate, but there's no sign of anyone.

I turn back towards the house and consider the situation. The intruder is busy trying to climb through the cat flap. He's big and the cat flap is small, and he looks funny with his back legs sticking straight out behind him!

Running up quickly, I take a satisfying swipe at his tail as he squirms around in the flap.

"*MEOW!*" he screeches. He quickly attempts a U-turn, but he's stuck and can only go forward. As he wriggles, trying even harder to get through, I have another jab, but only manage to catch a clawful of fur.

Now he's in my house! I peer through

the cat flap and see him crossing the kitchen towards the stairs. "Oh, no, you don't! I told you, that's *my* house and upstairs are *my* beds!" I cry.

There's nothing for it but to rattle through the cat flap after him. Big Black turns and looks at me, but doesn't stop. He bounds up the stairs two at a time. I wait at the bottom, thinking furiously. How can I get rid of him?

I hear him thumping and scratching around upstairs. He jumps on one bed and then another, trying them all for size. Now he's in my humans' room and I can hear him sniffing and snuffling at something. A few more knocks and some more sniffing, then he hurtles out of the bedroom with something held in his mouth.

Something large, brown and ... meaty. Before I've quite figured it out, he's flown down the stairs, past me and out through the cat flap.

Then it hits me – he's got my beef! The delicious piece of beef I've been waiting to give to my humans when they come home.

I race after him, across the kitchen and through the cat flap, but he's already at the gate. At that very moment it opens and he cannons straight into Mrs Browne, who is bringing me my dinner.

"Hey, that's my missing beef!" she shouts, dropping the food bowl and running after the intruder.

Quickly realising she'll never catch him, she turns back to find me investigating the spilled food. "I'm so sorry, Little Kitty," she says. "I actually thought *you'd* stolen my beef, but it turns out it was that horrible black creature all along."

Chapter Six

Now that the monster has gone and I've been found innocent of a crime - one that I did actually commit - it's time to put my acting skills to the test . . .

My humans think I'm asleep whenever I lie on top of the moving picture box they like to stare at but, in fact, I'm carefully studying what they're watching, looking for ideas.

For example, that pitiful, drawn-out

'meeeeow' I do when my food bowl is empty? I got my inspiration for that from a cat food advert.

And now I need to come up with something extra-special, to ensure Mrs Browne makes it up to me for suspecting me of theft. Never mind that it *was* me who stole the beef.

Which of my many, many dramatic performances shall I use? Aha! With a sudden flash of inspiration, I hold up a front paw and begin to limp slowly and painfully towards her, making my most heartbreaking mewling sound.

"Little Kitty!" she cries. "Poor thing. Did the nasty black cat hurt you when you were bravely trying to stop him running away with my beef?"

I look imploringly at her, eyes wide, holding up the 'poorly' paw. At the same time, I am trying to make her see that what I need most, what will make me feel better, is fish. A lot of fish.

Unfortunately, Mrs Browne is starting to look really worried. "Perhaps I should take you to the vet's," she says half to herself. "I'm not sure how we'd get there, but I think perhaps the number 11 bus goes near the surgery."

The vet's? Yikes, I think to myself. That is not at all what I wanted to happen! As if it wasn't bad enough having to wrestle that big black monster and being suspected of stealing beef – the vet's is the last place I want to go after all that.

I look as pointedly as I can at the spilled food she brought me, sniffing at it then looking up at her. My expression so clearly says 'You can't possibly expect a brave, wounded cat like me to eat food that has been on the floor, can you?'

"Poor Little Kitty," she says again. "Well, first it's time for your dinner. A cat as brave as you deserves a very special treat. You just wait here and try to keep out of danger while I run to the corner shop to see if they have any fresh salmon for you."

She finally got the message! I start to purr contentedly to myself. I've really hit the jackpot this time. Salmon! How wonderful! Of course, I know Mrs Browne won't exactly be running anywhere – she's not as young as she was – and I do feel a bit guilty for putting her to so much trouble. But the guilt only lasts for a moment.

"Salmon, salmon, salmon," I repeat to

myself, as Mrs Browne rushes away to do my bidding.

Then suddenly I hear a noise from the end of the garden. The black tomcat is back again, sitting on top of the fence!

"Salmon, eh?" he says with a sneer. "Salmon just happens to be my favourite food. So, Little Kitty, or whatever she called you, what are you going to do to stop me taking it?"

With that, he jumps down into the garden and stands in front of me, his jet-black fur all fluffed up and his back arched.

Chapter Seven

Oh my goodness! What do I do now? He's really big and mean and I am more than a little afraid.

I look at him more closely now and I see that he is either a stray or a cat that gets himself into a lot of trouble. His fur is matted and his tail has a kink in the middle. My tail is long and elegant, a thing of beauty. I swish it at him, trying to look as menacing as possible. But with a tail like this, it's hard to look anything but amazing.

"What do you think you're looking at?" he growls at me and I can see that he has some teeth missing, too. How on earth have I got myself into this situation? And where is Mrs Browne when I need her?

With a confident swagger that tells me he means business, Big Black begins moving closer to me. I need to protect the salmon at all costs! *My* salmon! Okay, technically it's Mrs Browne's salmon . . . if she ever gets back here with it!

Big Black is obviously intent on bullying me to get his own way. But I am not going to let him steal from me again! I'm just pondering how I can stop him when suddenly I hear a gruff voice.

"Oi! Thor! Get your furry backside back in the van!"

Thor? Really? I think.

The big cat looks startled and turns round as a large man with a scar on his chin and a walk that makes the earth shake heads past us. In his hand he has a crowbar and a large bag.

I wonder what he is going to do with those and why is he walking towards Mrs Browne's house - he's looking very shifty! I know I need to do something, and quickly, because I think this pair are after more than just salmon. It appears there is another type of cat burglar in the neighbourhood today . . .

Big Black, also known as Thor, apparently, bristles as the man stomps by. It seems he doesn't like being told what to do any more than I do! He turns to look at me again and hisses menacingly.

When the man reaches the house he looks around quickly to check that no one is watching, and then opens the back door. Ignoring the man's instructions to return to the van, Thor immediately darts into Mrs Browne's lovely home. He stares me through the kitchen window with what I can only describe as a sneer. Oh, the cheek of them, this cat and his human!

My tail starts to twitch with anger. Thor has already stolen from me once and there is no way I am going to let him and his human do the same to any of my humans! But what can I do? One little cat, all on her own? One very frightened little cat!

Chapter Eight

Well, what to do? I start by giving myself a stern talking to for being such a scaredy-cat, then I scratch my ear and begin to think. But I can't waste too much time thinking – action is what's needed.

The man has shut the back door, so I scramble up the tree next to Mrs Browne's house and then drop daintily through the kitchen window and down onto the worktop. I award myself a brownie point for poise.

No sign of Thor or his human. I stand still, cock my head to one side and listen. What's that banging and crashing? It's coming from Mrs Browne's sitting room. I jump down from the worktop and peer cautiously round the door. He's there, Thor's human, and he's stuffing his bag with Mrs Browne's lovely ornaments. How awful, stealing from an old lady! What a lowlife! My fur bristles with indignation.

As the man bends over, I gather myself and then leap onto his back. "Owww!" he roars as my sharp claws push through his jumper, through his shirt, and finally dig into his skin.

"Ouch! *Ouch!*" He tries to shake me off, twisting first one way and then the other. I grimly try to hang on, but I can't stop myself from slipping down his back and landing on the floor.

I quickly turn round and there's Thor, bigger and uglier than ever. He arches his back, bares what few teeth he has and spits at me. He makes a deep rumbling sound in his throat. I throw back my head and hiss at him rather unconvincingly. Although I puff up my fur and raise my tail like a warrior's spear, I am still only half his size. Thor licks his teeth ominously. If he doesn't get that salmon, I think he's going to tuck into me!

Suddenly, Thor pounces at me. Although he's heavier and stronger, I have dancer's blood in my veins, which makes me lighter and nimbler. He swipes and I dodge. He bites and I scratch. Then we're locked together, a giant ball of flying fur, rolling over and over on Mrs Browne's best Persian rug.

I taste blood. I just have time to wonder if it's mine or Thor's before everything goes black . . .

When I wake up I am lying on old Mrs Browne's lap. Out of the one eye I can open, I see her anxious face hovering over me. I try to utter a reassuring meow, but no sound comes out.

"Poor Little Kitty, brave Little Kitty, clever Little Kitty," she says, stroking me very, very gently. This time I do manage a squeak and the wrinkles on her face rearrange themselves as she smiles. "Oh, thank goodness," she cries. "And you should see that ugly brute. You added a torn ear to his collection of battle scars!"

I freeze at the mention of Big Black. Where is Thor? And his human?

"Don't worry," Mrs Browne says. "The cat and thief scooted out through the back door as soon as I arrived home and, apart from the mess, no harm has been done." I look around. The man's bag lies discarded on the floor, with Mrs Browne's prized possessions spilling out.

I lay back, paws waving, to enjoy Mrs Browne's soft, soothing strokes. I mean, really, what's not to like? Warmth, comfort, total adoration . . .but I feel that something's missing. My tummy rumbles loudly. I struggle to stand up, then I slide to the floor and begin tottering towards the kitchen, sniffing as I go.

Mrs Browne laughs. "Hungry are you, Little Kitty, after your ordeal? Well, the salmon is waiting for you."

I break into a trot.

The End

About the Authors

Tracy Terry

A Geordie lass, rumoured to have been born with a paperback in her hand, Tracy spends her days reading and reviewing books on her blog, Pen and Paper. A lover of hedgehogs as well as cats, she also enjoys writing and receiving letters and is quite the movie buff. Her taste in films is almost as eclectic as her taste in novels!

To find out more about Tracy, or to follow her on social media, visit:
www.pettywitter.blogspot.co.uk

Ann Bowyer

Ann is a retired Business Studies teacher. She has two sons and six grandchildren, and lives in Norfolk. After writing factual articles for magazines, Ann published her first fictional book in 2013. *A Token of Love*, which is based on the true story of her grandparents' lives, has sold all around the world. She was featured in an article in the *Hindu*, India's national paper, and, following numerous requests, is due to publish a sequel, *Lost in a Homeland*.

To find out more about Ann, or to follow her on social media, visit:

www.annbowyer.com

Suzan Collins

Suzan is an internationally selling author who writes in various genres, both fiction and non-fiction. Her non-fiction includes textbooks pertaining to her work as consultant and trainer in Social Care and Management. Suzan also writes fiction – naughty, spicy and otherwise – under the pen name Zina Adams.

Finalist – People's Book Prize, 2014

Shortlisted for *Best Achievement Award* – People's Book Prize, 2014

To find out more about Suzan, or to follow her on social media, visit:

www.suzancollins.com

Lucille Rayner

Lucille is a Support Worker and assists and supports older people. She loves holidays in the sunshine, family get-togethers and walking in the Suffolk countryside. Lucille enjoys writing in her spare time and is currently writing a children's book.

To find out more about Lucille, or to follow her on social media, visit:
www.facebook.com/pages/Lucille-Rayner/362171100645432?fref=ts

Jo Wilde

Jo was born in Yorkshire, many more years ago than she cares to remember. She works in a theatre and a library, and fills up the rest of her time reading, writing, editing, proofreading, event organising, eating chocolate and drinking wine.

To find out more about Jo, or to follow her on social media, visit:

www.scaryjojo.wordpress.com

Tottie Limejuice

Tottie Limejuice is one of the pen names of former journalist and copywriter Lesley Tottie. Lesley lives in France and now writes full-time. Her travel memoirs are published under the name Tottie Limejuice, and she also writes crime novels as L M Krier and children's books as L M Kay. Her interests include organic gardening, camping and walking with her two rescued border collies.

To find out more about Tottie, or to follow her on social media, visit:

www.tottielimejuice.com

JB Johnston

Known as JB Johnston in the bookish world – and sometimes, because she has a split personality, Debbie Johnston – JB is a book blogger and book tour coordinator, organising virtual book tours and other promotional work. She can be found over at her site Brook Cottage Books, and is a lifestyle reviewer for Loveahappyending.com and reviews for various other sites. Shortlisted in the 2013 Romance Industry Awards for Romance Blogger of the Year, JB is hoping to turn her love of books, writing and promotional work into a full-time career.

To find out more about JB,
or to follow her on social media, visit:
www.brookcottagebooks.blogspot.co.uk

Ros Lyons

Ros is interested in writing both fiction and memoirs. Her two cats provide much inspiration for creating stories. She belongs to two writing groups, where authors share their work and learn from each other. She enters the occasional writing competition and has had some success. As well as writing, Ros enjoys walking, the theatre and playing social bridge.

About the Artists

Catie Atkinson

Catie is an illustrator and designer based in Leeds. When she's not drawing, she enjoys reading, cooking, acting, singing in the choir and attempting to play various instruments – although not all at the same time! She also loves crime thrillers and is convinced that in another life she would have made a great detective!

To find out more about Catie, or to follow her on social media, visit:

www.catieatkinsonart.co.uk

Rachel Lawston

Rachel is a book designer who has worked with Penguin Random House, HarperCollins and Walker Books, to name a few. Rising to the challenge of designing books and commissioning artwork for amazing authors like Terry Pratchett, John Boyne and Malorie Blackman are some of her biggest accomplishments. She is a huge tortoise enthusiast, and is secretly hoping that at least one of the fantastic authors who took part in this project might base their next book on her two naughty Hermann's tortoises, Daenerys and Om . . .

To find out more about Rachel, or to follow her on social media, visit:

www.lawstondesign.com

About the Editor

Jaine Keskeys

Jaine is a Senior Editor who has worked in publishing for many years. She has written and edited projects for many fantastic publishers, including Penguin Random House and Egmont. Jaine spends her spare time reading and writing, and hopes to one day see her own picture books in print. Her beautiful nieces, Summer and Freya, and gorgeous nephew, Bryce, provide endless inspiration!

To find out more about Jaine, or to follow her on social media, visit:

www.editorjaine.com

Dear Reader,

If you have enjoyed reading this book, please tell all your friends and shout about it everywhere!

Please also leave a review on Amazon and Goodreads.

Thank you!

12380751R00037

Printed in Great Britain
by Amazon.co.uk, Ltd.,
Marston Gate.